Level E • Book 2

QuickReads®

A Research-Based Fluency Program

Elfrieda H. Hiebert, Ph.D.

MODERN CURRICULUM PRESS

Pearson Learning Group

Program Reviewers and Consultants

Dr. Barbara A. Baird
Director of Federal Programs/Richardson ISD
Richardson, TX

Dr. Kate Kinsella
Dept. of Secondary Education and Step to College Program
San Francisco State University
San Francisco, CA

Pat Sears
Early Child Coordinator/Virginia Beach Public Schools
Virginia Beach, VA

Dr. Judith B. Smith
Supervisor of ESOL and World and Classical Languages/Baltimore City Public Schools
Baltimore, MD

The following people have contributed to the development of this product:

Art and Design: David Mager, Salita Mehta, Evelyn O'Shea, Dan Thomas, Dan Trush, Karolyn Wehner

Editorial: Lynn W. Kloss

Manufacturing: Michele Uhl

Marketing: Alison Bruno

Production: Jeffrey Engel, Roxanne Knoll, Phyllis Rosinsky

Publishing Operations: Jennifer Van Der Heide

Modern Curriculum Press
Pearson Learning Group

1-800-321-3106
www.pearsonlearning.com

Contents

Contents

SCIENCE **Minerals**

Contents

SOCIAL STUDIES

The World's Population

SOCIAL
STUDIES

Rivers of the United States

Contents

Acknowledgments

All photography © Pearson Education, Inc. (PEI) unless otherwise specifically noted.

Cover: Courtesy, Kennedy Space Center/NASA. 3: © Galen Rowell/Corbis. 4: James Randklev/Stone/Getty Images. 5: © Alen MacWeeney/Corbis. 6: Las Vegas News Bureau/LVCVA. 7: Getty Images, Inc. 10: © Galen Rowell/Corbis. 12: Jeff Newbery. 14: © Mark L. Stephenson/Corbis. 16: © Bettmann/Corbis. 18: *t.* NASA; *b.l.* Florence Museo delle Scienze/AKG London; *b.r.* © Bettmann/Corbis. 26: © Steve Skjold/Skjold Photography. 28: James Randklev/Stone/Getty Images. 30: Bob Winsett/Index Stock Imagery/PictureQuest. 32: © Nik Wheeler/Corbis. 40: *l.* Stephen Frisch/Stock Boston; *m.* Aaron Haupt/Photo Researchers, Inc; r. Breck P. Kent/Breck P. Kent Photography. 42: © Alen MacWeeney/Corbis. 44: Richard H. Johnston/Getty Images, Inc. 46: *l.* Rene Macura/AP/Wide World Photo; r. © Jonathan Blair/Corbis. 52: Las Vegas News Bureau/LVCVA. 66: Getty Images, Inc. 68: © Neil Rabinowitz/Corbis. 70: John Beatty/Stone/Getty Images. 72: bkgd. © Marc Garanger/Corbis; inset © Lester Lefkowitz/Corbis. 74: John Eastcott/Yva Momatiuk/Photo Researchers, Inc. 80: © Kindra Clineff/Index Stock Imagery/PictureQuest. 86: Michael Newman/PhotoEdit/PictureQuest. 88: David Young-Wolff/Stone/Getty Images.

Earth's Moon

The Moon looks much smaller than these mountains because it is far away from Earth.

Earth's Satellite

Of the many bodies in the solar system, the Moon is the closest to Earth. Because it is almost 239,000 miles from Earth,[25] the Moon looks small. However, even at one-quarter the size of Earth, the Moon is large.

The Moon regularly appears in the night sky[50] because it is a satellite of Earth. A satellite moves around a larger body. As Earth's satellite, the Moon travels around Earth and goes along[75] with Earth as it orbits the Sun.

While it travels with Earth, the Moon rotates on its axis. Earth rotates on its own axis, too.[100] Because of the timing of the rotations of the Moon and Earth, one side of the Moon is never seen from Earth. This side is called "the far side of the Moon."[132]

The picture on the top shows the Bay of Fundy at low tide.
The picture on the bottom shows the Bay of Fundy at high tide.

The Moon and Tides

Visitors to the ocean know that the level of the water at a beach changes throughout the day. At low tide,[25] you see a lot of sand. At high tide, much of the sand is covered by water.

Tides are largely caused by the Moon. The[50] Moon's gravity pulls slightly on the oceans, causing the oceans to rise. In this way, the force of the Moon's gravity causes the rising and[75] falling of tides.

The height of tides depends on the shape of the coastline and the depth of the ocean. The highest tides on Earth[100] occur in the Bay of Fundy, which borders the Atlantic Ocean in Canada. The height of the Atlantic Ocean in the Bay of Fundy increases by as much as 53 feet during high tide.[134]

Earth's Moon

In this picture, you can see only a small part of the Moon.

A Moon Month

The Moon seems to give off light, but it does not. Instead, it reflects the Sun's light. The Moon's size seems to^{25} change over a month, but it does not. What changes is the amount of the Moon that is visible from Earth as the Moon orbits^{50} around Earth. Over a month, the Moon goes through different lunar phases.

The lunar phases begin with the new Moon, when only a sliver of^{75} the Moon is visible. Over the next two weeks, the Moon seems to increase in size, or wax. The full moon, which appears as a^{100} round ball, happens when the Moon is halfway around Earth. Over the next two weeks, the Moon seems to shrink, or wane, until only a sliver is visible. Then, the lunar phases start again.^{134}

Earth's Moon

In this picture, astronaut John W. Young walks on the Moon.

Humans on the Moon

From 1969 to 1972, 12 American astronauts visited the Moon. Because the Moon poses challenges for humans, the astronauts had to[25] prepare for their trip. The Moon does not have oxygen, food, or water, so the astronauts had to bring these things. Plants can't grow on[50] the Moon because the Moon doesn't have oxygen. The Moon also doesn't have oceans or lakes, but it does have ice at its North and[75] South Poles. However, this ice would be difficult for humans to get and use.

The astronauts also prepared for the challenge of walking on the[100] Moon. The Moon's gravity is one-sixth that of Earth. Because humans weigh much less on the Moon, they bounce rather than walk. The astronauts had to learn to walk in the Moon's gravity.[134]

Galileo and his telescope are shown with the four Galilean moons.

The Moons of Other Planets

Earth's Moon is only one of at least 100 known moons in the solar system. Nearly all of our solar[25] system's moons orbit around the four large outer planets. The largest planet, Jupiter, has at least 52 moons.

Most of Jupiter's moons are small. However,[50] the four Galilean moons are large. The Galilean moons were named after the astronomer Galileo, who was the first person to use a telescope to[75] study outer space. Although Galileo's telescope was not powerful, he saw Jupiter's four large moons.

Astronomers are very interested in a Galilean moon called Europa.[100] They believe that an ocean lies beneath the ice that covers Europa. This ocean is the only place in the solar system, other than Earth, that astronomers think could have the conditions for life.[134]

Earth's Moon

Write words that will help you remember what you learned.

Earth's Satellite

_____

_____

_____

_____

The Moon and Tides

_____

_____

_____

_____

A Moon Month

_____

_____

_____

_____

Humans on the Moon

_____

_____

_____

_____

The Moons of Other Planets

_____

_____

_____

_____

Earth's Satellite

1. Around what two bodies does the Moon orbit?

   Ⓐ the Sun and a star

   Ⓑ Earth and the Sun

   Ⓒ a satellite and a planet

   Ⓓ Earth and the solar system

2. Why is the Moon said to be a satellite of Earth?

   _____

   _____

   _____

The Moon and Tides

1. What is one cause of the tides in Earth's oceans?

   Ⓐ the Moon's gravity pulling on the oceans

   Ⓑ how much sand is on the ocean beaches

   Ⓒ the amount of water in the Atlantic Ocean

   Ⓓ Earth's gravity pulling on the oceans

2. What two things do the height of the tides depend on?

   _____

   _____

   _____

Earth's Moon

A Moon Month

1. Why does the Moon's size seem to change over a month?

    Ⓐ The amount of the Moon that is visible from Earth changes.

    Ⓑ The moon's size decreases as it moves away from Earth.

    Ⓒ The moon is always visible when the lunar phases start.

    Ⓓ The moon's size increases as it moves toward the Sun.

2. What are the lunar phases?

    _____

    _____

    _____

Humans on the Moon

1. The main idea of "Humans on the Moon" is _____

    Ⓐ how astronauts were chosen to go to the Moon.

    Ⓑ how astronauts learned to walk on the Moon.

    Ⓒ how astronauts found oxygen and water on the Moon.

    Ⓓ the challenges astronauts face on the Moon.

2. What are three things the astronauts had to bring to the Moon to survive?

    _____

    _____

    _____

The Moons of Other Planets

1. "The Moons of Other Planets" is MAINLY about _____

    Ⓐ the moons in our solar system.

    Ⓑ the moons of Jupiter and Europa.

    Ⓒ finding life on other planets.

    Ⓓ how Galileo discovered the Galilean moons.

2. Why are astronomers interested in Europa?

    _____

    _____

    _____

Connect Your Ideas

1. What are three things you have learned about Earth's Moon?

    _____

    _____

    _____

2. What are two things that astronauts might learn from visiting the Moon?

    _____

    _____

    _____

Air and the Atmosphere

The Atmosphere of Earth

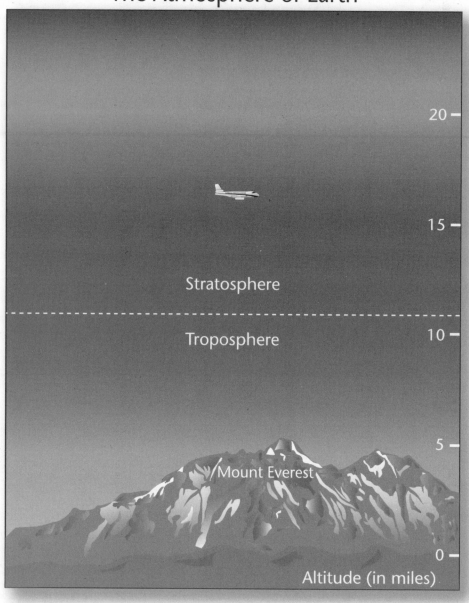

This drawing shows two of the layers of Earth's atmosphere.

Earth's Atmosphere

The atmosphere is like a blanket of air covering Earth. This blanket of air is about 300 miles thick. Air is a mixture [25] of oxygen, carbon dioxide, and small amounts of other gases. Earth's atmosphere has the only air in the solar system.

Air is thickest close to [50] Earth's surface and thins out higher in the atmosphere. The first of the five layers of the atmosphere is called the troposphere. Three-quarters of [75] Earth's air is in the troposphere, even though the troposphere extends only 11 miles from Earth's surface.

The second layer of air is called the [100] stratosphere. The stratosphere contains a form of oxygen called ozone. Ozone absorbs most of the Sun's ultraviolet rays. Without the ozone in the stratosphere, the Sun's ultraviolet rays would harm living things on Earth. [134]

Air and the Atmosphere

The boy in this picture is fixing a bike tire. The air pressure inside and outside tires helps bikes move.

Air Pressure

Even though air cannot be seen, it has weight. The weight of air presses down on the surface of Earth and on everything[25] on Earth. As it presses down, air applies about the same pressure everywhere.

Air pressure is measured in pounds per square inch. A square inch[50] is about the size of a small postage stamp. Air pressure is about 14.7 pounds per square inch. This means that air applies a force[75] of about 14.7 pounds on every square inch of everything it touches.

People do not collapse from the weight of air on them because of[100] the air that is inside their bodies. The air in a person's lungs applies enough pressure inside the body to balance the air pressure on the outside of the body.[130]

Air and the Atmosphere

The hot gas in these balloons lets them fly high in the air.

Sports and Air

Things that are lighter than air, such as a balloon filled with hot gas, float in air. Things that are heavier than [25] air, such as a soccer ball, fall to the ground. These features of air make some games and sports possible.

A basketball bounces when air [50] is compressed, or squeezed into it. Without compressed air, a basketball stays on the ground and can't be bounced. When compressed air is added to [75] tires, bicycles can be ridden for miles.

Other games and sports use moving air, or wind. With wind, a kite flies through the sky. Without [100] wind, a kite stays on the ground. Windsurfing is a sport that uses wind. Windsurfers stand on long surfboards and move sails to catch the wind, which speeds them across the water. [132]

Air and the Atmosphere

Skiers need to adjust to high altitudes so that they can ski safely.

Air and Elevation

A place's elevation is its distance above sea level. The elevation of ocean beaches is about zero. The city of Santa Fe,[25] New Mexico, has an elevation of 7,000 feet above sea level. Because air has less oxygen at higher elevations, breathing is more difficult in Santa[50] Fe than at the ocean.

Many mountains where people ski have elevations of 8,000 feet or more. Air has $\frac{1}{4}$ less oxygen at 8,000 feet[75] than it does at sea level. Skiers need to adjust to the thinner air at high elevations before they can ski safely.

Although large airplanes[100] fly at 20,000 to 40,000 feet above sea level, people can breathe comfortably. This is because large airplanes use a pump to keep air pressure inside the plane at a comfortable level for breathing.[135]

Air and the Atmosphere

Harmful chemicals, such as fumes from cars,
can pollute the air and make it hard to breathe.
This picture shows pollution in Los Angeles.

Clean Air

You are breathing air that someone else breathed a minute ago. A year from now, someone on the other side of the world[25] will breathe the air you just breathed. People, animals, and plants use the same air again and again.

While the amount of air in the[50] atmosphere stays the same, the mixture of gases in the air changes. Fumes from cars, oven cleaners, and nail polish can add harmful chemicals[75] to the air. If too many harmful chemicals are added, air becomes polluted. Polluted air can be unsafe for people, animals, and plants to breathe.[100]

Plants balance gases in the air by taking in carbon dioxide and giving off oxygen. In this way, large forests help to keep the right balance of carbon dioxide and oxygen in the air.[134]

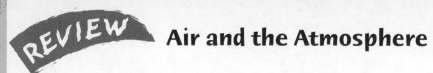

Air and the Atmosphere

Write words that will help you remember what you learned.

Earth's Atmosphere

_____

_____

_____

_____

Air Pressure

_____

_____

_____

_____

Sports and Air

_____

_____

_____

_____

Air and Elevation

_____

_____

_____

_____

Clean Air

_____

_____

_____

_____

Earth's Atmosphere

1. What does ozone do?

   (A) It increases the amount of oxygen in the air.

   (B) It absorbs the Sun's ultraviolet rays.

   (C) It absorbs the air in the troposphere.

   (D) Its rays harm living things on Earth.

2. What is Earth's atmosphere?

   _____

   _____

   _____

Air Pressure

1. Which of these statements is a fact you learned in "Air Pressure"?

   (A) Air applies more pressure on the ocean than on land.

   (B) Air pressure is only in people's lungs.

   (C) Air does not apply pressure on people.

   (D) Air pressure is about the same everywhere on Earth.

2. Why don't people collapse from the weight of air?

   _____

   _____

   _____

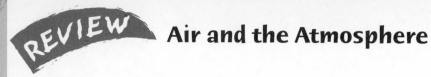

REVIEW **Air and the Atmosphere**

Sports and Air

1. "Sports and Air" is MAINLY about _____

   Ⓐ sports that use balls and surfboards.

   Ⓑ why wind is important to sports.

   Ⓒ why basketballs and soccer balls need air.

   Ⓓ how air is used in sports in different ways.

2. How does compressed air help people play some sports?

   _____

   _____

   _____

Air and Elevation

1. Why is it difficult to breathe in the mountains?

   Ⓐ There is less oxygen.

   Ⓑ There is more oxygen.

   Ⓒ The elevation is low.

   Ⓓ There is more atmosphere.

2. What is elevation?

   _____

   _____

   _____

Clean Air

1. How do plants help people breathe clean air?

   (A) Plants change the amount of air in the atmosphere.

   (B) Plants balance the amount of pollution in the air.

   (C) Plants balance the carbon dioxide and oxygen in the air.

   (D) Plants keep people and animals from breathing too much air.

2. How can the mixture of gases in the air be dangerous?

   _____

   _____

   _____

Connect Your Ideas

1. What are three things you learned about air in these passages?

   _____

   _____

   _____

2. Describe two ways in which you use air every day.

   _____

   _____

   _____

Minerals

People need the mineral calcium, which is found in milk and leafy green vegetables, to stay healthy.

What Are Minerals?

Rocks are made of minerals. Minerals are things that are found in nature but have never been alive. Each kind of mineral[25] has its own crystal pattern and makeup. Although rocks usually contain several different minerals, they sometimes contain only one.

More than 4,000 minerals have been[50] identified, each with its own properties, such as hardness or shine. Among the identified minerals, only 20 are common. Two minerals, feldspar and quartz, make[75] up most of Earth's crust.

Minerals are everywhere in nature and in products made by people—from buildings and cars to watches and pencils. People[100] need minerals, such as calcium, too. Although calcium is also found in chalk and pearls, it is the calcium found in milk and leafy green vegetables that keeps people healthy.[130]

Minerals

Earth has many different kinds of minerals. Shown here from left to right are purple quartz, azurite, and talc.

Properties of Minerals

Each mineral has special traits, or properties, that make it different from other minerals. Some minerals can be identified by color. The[25] mineral azurite was named for its color, which is azure, or sky blue. Although azurite is always blue, many other minerals are found in different[50] colors. For example, quartz can be purple, yellow, or pink.

Even if a mineral has several colors, however, the powder it makes when it is[75] crushed is always the same color. For example, the mineral hematite looks black, but the powder of hematite is always red.

Another property of minerals[100] is how easily they can be scratched. The easiest mineral to scratch is talc, which is used in powder. In contrast, diamonds, which are the hardest mineral, can scratch all other minerals.[132]

Minerals

This picture shows the many different shapes that crystals form.

Crystals

The salt that we put on food is made up of small crystals. Most minerals can be found in nature in crystal form. Although[25] the crystals of each mineral always have the same shape, this shape depends on the chemicals in the mineral. Some chemicals create crystals that are[50] shaped like cubes, diamonds, or other more complex forms. Over long periods of time and with the right conditions, crystals form naturally in Earth.

People[75] have also learned to make crystals. These synthetic crystals, or crystals made by people, take much less time to develop than natural crystals. Synthetic silicon[100] crystals have played a big part in developing satellites, spacecraft, and computers. Tiny slices or chips of silicon crystals are used to build the circuits that make satellites, spacecraft, and computers run.[132]

This worker is pouring hot metal into a mold.

Metals

Cars, soft-drink cans, forks, and thousands of other products are made with metal. Except for a handful of metals, such as gold and [25] silver, metals are found only in ores. Ores are minerals that contain metal. Once ores are mined from Earth, the mineral has to be heated [50] to a very high temperature to remove the metal.

Most metals allow electricity and heat to flow through them easily. In addition, metals can be [75] shaped when heated. These properties make metals very useful.

Soft metals, such as iron, can often be strengthened by mixing them with another metal. The [100] new metal mixture is called an alloy. Steel is an alloy that is produced by mixing carbon and iron. Buildings are often made of steel because it is so strong. [130]

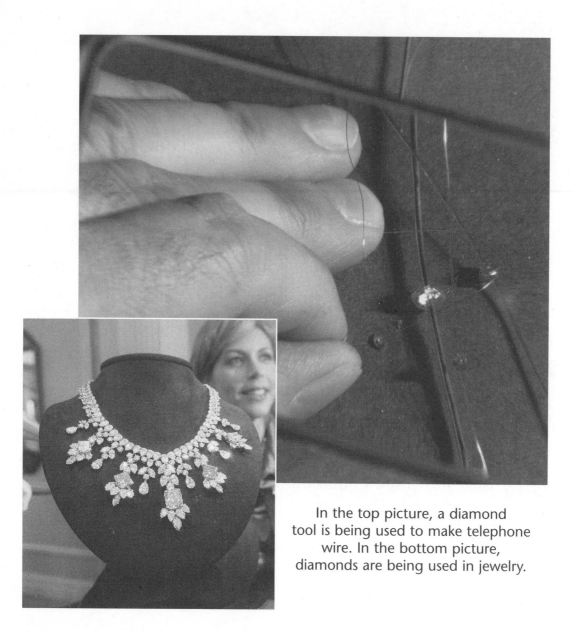

In the top picture, a diamond tool is being used to make telephone wire. In the bottom picture, diamonds are being used in jewelry.

Gemstones

Minerals such as diamonds and rubies are called precious stones, or gemstones, because they are rare and beautiful. The crystals of most minerals are[25] tiny and packed together tightly. However, gemstones usually come from single, large crystals.

Large crystals form only under certain conditions. For example, diamonds are formed[50] from carbon that has been kept at a high temperature and under great pressure inside Earth for a long time. With less pressure and a[75] lower temperature, carbon forms graphite, which is the lead in pencils.

Gemstones are also valued because they are hard. Although the graphite in pencils wears[100] down easily, diamonds are the hardest known substance. Only a diamond drill can cut diamonds. Because of their strength, diamonds have many uses. Some of the tools that doctors use even have diamond blades.[134]

Write words that will help you remember what you learned.

What Are Minerals?

_____

_____

_____

_____

Properties of Minerals

_____

_____

_____

_____

Crystals

_____

_____

_____

_____

Metals

_____

_____

_____

_____

Gemstones

_____

_____

_____

_____

What Are Minerals?

1. Which of the following BEST describes minerals?

    Ⓐ things found in nature that were never alive

    Ⓑ the calcium in Earth's crust

    Ⓒ rocks with crystal patterns that keep changing

    Ⓓ things found in nature that were once living

2. What are two ways people use minerals?

_____

_____

_____

Properties of Minerals

1. "Properties of Minerals" is MAINLY about _____

    Ⓐ how to identify a mineral by its color.

    Ⓑ why minerals are found in so many places on Earth.

    Ⓒ how minerals are different from one another.

    Ⓓ ways in which people use minerals.

2. What are two properties of minerals?

_____

_____

_____

Crystals

1. Which of the following is a fact about crystals?

   Ⓐ All crystals are the same color.

   Ⓑ The crystals of each mineral always have the same shape.

   Ⓒ It takes longer for people to make crystals than for them to be made in Earth.

   Ⓓ The silicon crystals used in computers are found in Earth.

2. What is one difference between crystals found in Earth and crystals that are made by people?

   _____

   _____

   _____

Metals

1. Which of the following is a fact about metals?

   Ⓐ Most metals allow heat and electricity to flow through them.

   Ⓑ All metals are shiny and have the same color and shape.

   Ⓒ Most metals are alloys that are mined from Earth.

   Ⓓ All metals are soft until they are mixed with minerals and ores.

2. What are alloys and ores?

   _____

   _____

   _____

Gemstones

1. Another good name for "Gemstones" is _____

   Ⓐ "How Pencils Are Made."

   Ⓑ "Crystals to Wear."

   Ⓒ "Precious Stones."

   Ⓓ "Diamonds and Rubies."

2. What are two reasons gemstones are valued?

   _____

   _____

   _____

Connect Your Ideas

1. Choose two of the minerals you read about in these passages and tell how they are alike and how they are different.

   _____

   _____

   _____

2. What are three ways we use minerals in everyday life?

   _____

   _____

   _____

The World's Population

The picture on the top shows Las Vegas, Nevada, in 1970. The picture on the bottom shows Las Vegas in the late 1990s. These pictures show you how much the city's population grew in less than 30 years.

Why Is Population Important?

Any place where people live has a population. The population of a place is the number of people who live there.[25] Cities, states, countries, and the world all have populations.

Populations change as people move, are born, and die. Those in charge of services, such as[50] schools and electricity, need to know about population changes.

In the last 10 years, Las Vegas, Nevada, has almost doubled in size. If scientists had[75] not been studying this change in population, Las Vegas, Nevada, might not have had enough electricity during its hot summers.

Scientists study the ages of[100] people in a population, too. If many families with children move to Las Vegas, Nevada, for example, new schools should be built. If the new people are senior citizens, different services are needed.[133]

The World's Population

Population of Earth

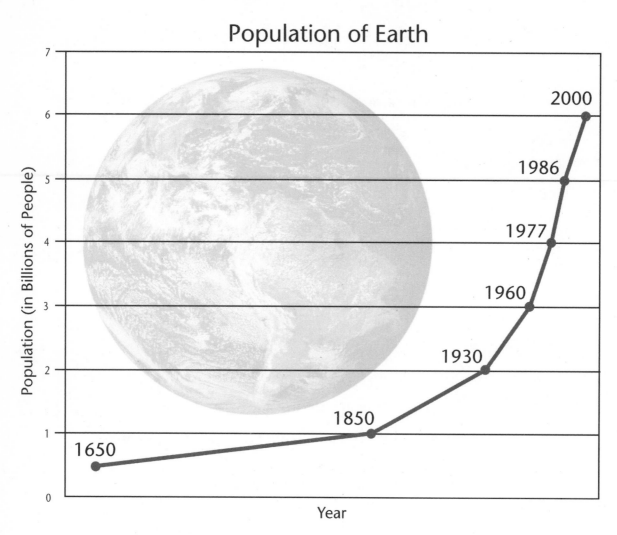

This line graph shows how much more quickly the world's population has grown in the last 150 years than it did in earlier years.

Populations Then and Now

The line graph that you see shows how the world's population has changed since 1650. In that year, the world had[25] about a half-billion people. It took another 200 years, until 1850, for the world's population to reach 1 billion. After 1850, the world's population[50] grew rapidly. By 2002, there were 6.3 billion people in the world.

The world's population has increased rapidly in the last 150 years because of[75] improved living conditions and farming methods. People have learned the importance of drinking clean water. When people get sick, better medicines are available. Farmers have[100] learned how to grow larger amounts of food. However, many of the world's 6.3 billion people still live in poor, crowded conditions and do not have enough medicine and food available to them.[133]

The World's Population

Places People Live in the World

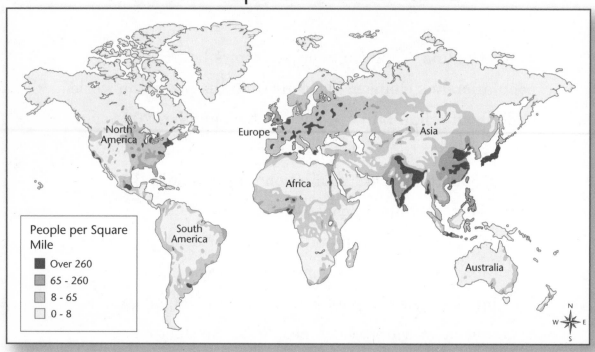

The box in the lower corner shows you how to use the colors on the map to learn which areas of the world are most heavily populated.

Where in the World Do People Live?

The map that you see shows where Earth's 6.3 billion people live. The dark parts show areas that[25] are heavily populated. The lighter parts show areas that are less populated.

More than half of Earth's population lives on the continent of Asia. India[50] and China, which are two countries on the continent of Asia, have more than one billion people each. Many people in these two countries live[75] in cities. China has 11 cities with 3 million people or more. The United States has only two cities as large: New York City and[100] Los Angeles.

Greenland is the country with the fewest number of people. Greenland has one person for every square mile of land. In contrast, India has 884 people for every square mile of land.[134]

The World's Population

Population of the United States in 2000

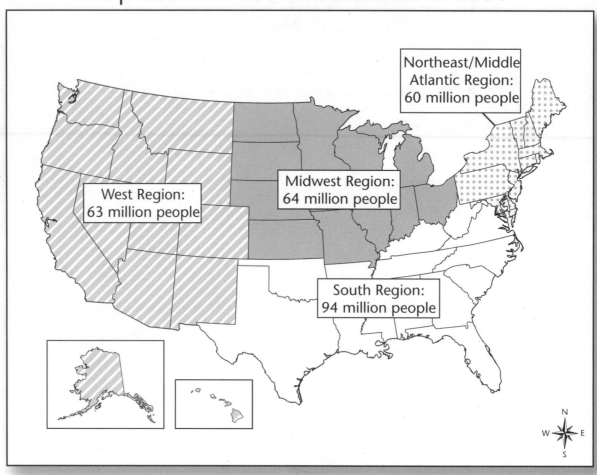

The boxes on the map show you how many people live in the four regions of the United States.

Where in the United States Do People Live?

Every 10 years, a count, or census, shows the population of the United States. In 2000, the[25] census counted 281 million Americans. The map that you see shows where these people live.

The South region has the most people: 94 million. The[50] West, Midwest, and Northeast regions each have about 60 million people. Although their populations are not too different in number, the regions are very different[75] in size.

The West is 10 times bigger than the Northeast but has 10 times fewer people per square mile. Many people in the Northeast[100] live in cities like New York City. In Alaska and other areas of the West, most people live on farms or in small towns. However, the West also has cities like Los Angeles.[133]

The World's Population

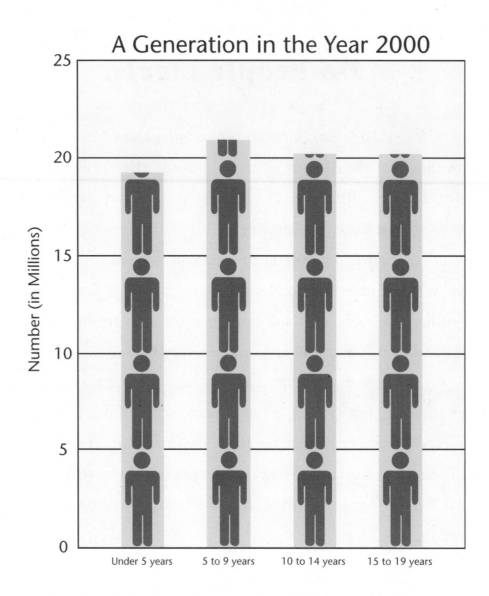

A Generation in the Year 2000

Each bar in this chart shows numbers in millions. That means that the first bar shows that there were about 18 million children who were under 5 years old in the year 2000.

A Generation of American Children

Everyone is part of a family, a town, and a country. In addition, everyone is part of a generation. Everyone[25] who is born in a certain time period is in the same generation.

You are part of a generation, too. The Census of 2000 counted[50] the number of children in your generation. The bar graph that you see shows that this census counted about 80 million children from preschool to[75] age 19. The bars on the chart show that each age group had about 20 million children. The 20 million children in your group will[100] finish school and get jobs at about the same time.

Some generations have nicknames. Your grandparents' generation is called the "baby boomers." Some day, your generation may have a nickname, too.[131]

REVIEW   The World's Population

Write words that will help you remember what you learned.

Why Is Population Important?

_____

_____

_____

_____

Populations Then and Now

_____

_____

_____

_____

Where in the World Do People Live?

_____

_____

_____

_____

Where in the United States Do People Live?

_____

_____

_____

_____

A Generation of American Children

_____

_____

_____

_____

Why Is Population Important?

1. "Why Is Population Important?" is MAINLY about _____

    Ⓐ why populations live in cities.

    Ⓑ why it is important to study population changes.

    Ⓒ why populations move from one place to another.

    Ⓓ why scientists study the population of Las Vegas, Nevada.

2. Why is it important for governments to know when populations change?

    _____

    _____

    _____

Populations Then and Now

1. The main idea of "Populations Then and Now" is that _____

    Ⓐ people today have enough medicine and food available to them.

    Ⓑ the world's population is growing too quickly today.

    Ⓒ people in 1650 did not have enough water and food.

    Ⓓ there are several reasons for the world's rapid growth in population.

2. What are two reasons the world's population has increased rapidly in the last 150 years?

    _____

    _____

    _____

The World's Population

Where in the World Do People Live?

1. More than half of the world's population lives _____

   Ⓐ in North and South America.

   Ⓑ on the continent of Africa.

   Ⓒ in India and the United States.

   Ⓓ on the continent of Asia.

2. What do the dark and light parts of the map on page 56 show?

   _____

   _____

   _____

Where in the United States Do People Live?

1. "Where in the United States Do People Live?" is MAINLY about _____

   Ⓐ where people live in the West region.

   Ⓑ how the regions of the United States are different.

   Ⓒ how the Census of 2000 was taken in the United States.

   Ⓓ why the United States counts its population every 10 years.

2. Compare the population and land of the West region to the population and land of the Northeast.

   _____

   _____

   _____

A Generation of American Children

1. Look at the chart on page 60. Which was the largest group of children?

   Ⓐ the group that was under 5 years old

   Ⓑ the group that was from 5 to 9 years old

   Ⓒ the group that was from 10 to 14 years old

   Ⓓ the group that was from 15 to 19 years old

2. What does it mean to be in the same generation as someone else?

   _____

   _____

   _____

Connect Your Ideas

1. Why might it be important to know how many people live in an area and where those people live?

   _____

   _____

   _____

2. Suppose there was another passage in this unit. Would you expect it to be about the foods of different countries or about how to take a census? Why?

   _____

   _____

   _____

Rivers of the United States

Many kinds of animals live in or near rivers, or find food there.

What Is a River?

A river is a body of water that can flow over or under land. Most rivers start in hills and mountains[25] where snow melts. Trickles of water flow downhill, forming a stream of water. Soon, several streams join to form a small river. Small rivers can[50] be tributaries, or arms, of larger rivers. In time, the largest river that the tributaries joins flows into the ocean.

Rivers provide environments for hundreds[75] of kinds of plants and animals. Many different kinds of fish swim in rivers. Different kinds of insects, birds, and animals live in the trees[100] and grasses that grow along the banks of rivers. Leaves from trees fall into the river and help to form the mud on river bottoms, where worms, snails, and other animals live.[132]

Rivers of the United States

Settlers often located cities on or near
rivers to make transportation easier.

Rivers and People

Rivers are important to people, animals, and plants. Many American cities, including New York and Los Angeles, are located near rivers. Settlers[25] chose locations by rivers because rivers provided water for drinking and for irrigating farmland. Before trains, planes, and highways were invented, people and goods were[50] transported on rivers more easily than on roads.

Rivers have not been used as much for transportation since planes, trains, and highways were invented. However,[75] rivers remain important to people. Ocean water is salty. But because most river water is fresh, people can use river water for drinking and for[100] irrigating farmland. People also use rivers for recreation. Many people enjoy rafting and fishing in rivers. Also, the animals and plants around rivers make them perfect locations for other kinds of recreation, including hiking.[134]

Rivers of the United States

Waterfalls, like this one in Yellowstone National Park,
create a spectacular landscape.

Rivers and Landscape

Fast-flowing water full of soil and rocks can change the landscape. Rivers have created spectacular landscapes, including the Grand Canyon and [25] Niagara Falls.

Cliffs and valleys form when rivers, such as the Colorado River, cut into land. Over thousands of years, the Colorado River cut through [50] layered rock to make the Grand Canyon. The Grand Canyon is 277 miles long, 18 miles wide at its widest, and one mile deep at [75] its deepest point.

A waterfall occurs when a river drops over a cliff. The outflow from four of the Great Lakes empties into the Niagara [100] River. This water pours over Niagara Falls on its way to the fifth Great Lake. At Niagara Falls, the river makes a spectacular drop that is about the height of a 20-story building. [134]

Rivers of the United States

The picture on the top shows that the Hoover Dam holds back a large lake. The picture on the bottom shows how high the Hoover Dam is.

Dams on Rivers

All of the major rivers in the United States have been changed by dams. A dam is a barrier built across a[25] river. The barrier holds water back, forming a lake or reservoir. When it is released from the reservoir, the water flows over the dam like[50] a waterfall. This action can generate electricity.

Generating electricity is only one reason dams are built. Reservoirs provide people with a steady supply of drinking[75] water. When rivers grow with melting snow in spring, dams can prevent flooding by holding back the extra water.

While dams help people in many[100] ways, they can also hurt the environment. Fish that live in a river lose the places where they lay eggs. The wetlands beside rivers, where many animals and plants live, can disappear as well.[134]

Rivers of the United States

This picture shows how high the Great Flood of 1993 was in Iowa.

The Mighty Mississippi

The Mississippi River, the longest river in North America, is called the Mighty Mississippi. The Mississippi and its tributaries, the Missouri and[25] the Ohio Rivers, form the world's third largest river system.

The Mississippi River starts near the Canadian border and flows south through 10 states to[50] the Gulf of Mexico. Its tributaries, the Missouri and Ohio, flow through another 21 states.

In 1993, the reason for the nickname Mighty Mississippi became[75] clear. Levees have been built along the Mississippi to hold back floods. After heavy rains in 1993, more than 1,000 levees failed along the upper[100] Mississippi and Missouri Rivers. Towns and farmland in nine Midwest states were covered with water and mud. Because of the size of the flood, this event was called the Great Flood of 1993.[133]

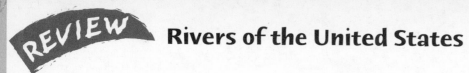

Rivers of the United States

Write words that will help you remember what you learned.

What Is a River?

_____

_____

_____

_____

Rivers and People

_____

_____

_____

_____

Rivers and Landscape

_____

_____

_____

_____

Dams on Rivers

_____

_____

_____

_____

The Mighty Mississippi

_____

_____

_____

_____

What Is a River?

1. "What Is a River?" is MAINLY about _____

    Ⓐ the many kinds of rivers in the United States.

    Ⓑ how rivers form and what lives in and around them.

    Ⓒ how streams form tributaries of rivers.

    Ⓓ the different kinds of animals that live near rivers.

2. How does the water from melting snow get to the ocean?

_____

_____

_____

Rivers and People

1. Settlers chose locations by rivers because it was easy to _____

    Ⓐ transport goods on rivers.

    Ⓑ go to the ocean on rivers.

    Ⓒ find locations for hiking near rivers.

    Ⓓ go to New York and Los Angeles on rivers.

2. What are two reasons rivers are important to people today?

_____

_____

_____

Rivers and Landscape

1. The main idea of "Rivers and Landscape" is that _____

   Ⓐ the Grand Canyon was formed by a river.

   Ⓑ rivers can change the landscape.

   Ⓒ water flows quickly in rivers.

   Ⓓ waterfalls made the Great Lakes.

2. Retell what you learned about how the Grand Canyon was produced.

   _____

   _____

   _____

Dams on Rivers

1. Dams can be helpful to people by _____

   Ⓐ giving fish places to live and lay eggs.

   Ⓑ forming reservoirs and rivers.

   Ⓒ generating electricity and providing drinking water.

   Ⓓ causing flooding and generating waterfalls.

2. How can dams hurt fish, plants, and animals?

   _____

   _____

   _____

The Mighty Mississippi

1. Another good name for "The Mighty Mississippi" is _____

    Ⓐ "The Midwest's Great River."

    Ⓑ "The Great Flood of 1993."

    Ⓒ "The Mississippi and the Gulf of Mexico."

    Ⓓ "The World's Largest River System."

2. What was the Great Flood of 1993?

    _____

    _____

    _____

Connect Your Ideas

1. Tell about three things rivers can provide.

    _____

    _____

    _____

2. Suppose there was another passage in this unit. Would you expect it to be about how to prevent floods in the United States or about the rivers of China? Why?

    _____

    _____

    _____

Managing Money

Budgets help people manage money
so they can buy birthday presents.

Budgets

A budget is a system for managing money. Families, schools, and businesses all have budgets. Individuals, including children, have budgets, too. The only difference[25] between budgets for individuals and budgets for businesses is their size. No matter what size they are, though, all budgets have the same two parts.[50]

One part of a budget is a record of income, or money coming in. A child's income might include money earned for doing jobs at[75] home or for neighbors. The other part of a budget is a record of expenses, or money going out. A child's expenses might include snacks[100] or presents for birthdays.

Individuals and businesses use budgets to manage their money. Records of income and expenses show people if they have money to buy things they need or want.[131]

Managing Money

Jamie's Budget

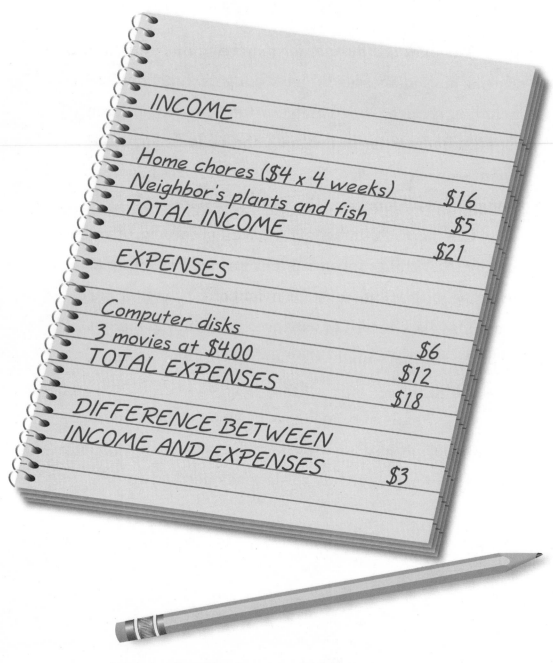

INCOME

Home chores ($4 x 4 weeks)	$16
Neighbor's plants and fish	$5
TOTAL INCOME	$21

EXPENSES

Computer disks	$6
3 movies at $4.00	$12
TOTAL EXPENSES	$18

DIFFERENCE BETWEEN INCOME AND EXPENSES — $3

Jamie has listed her income and expenses so that she can save money for a birthday gift for her mother.

Making a Budget

The budget that you see shows Jamie's income and expenses for one month. Her income of $21 came from taking care of [25] a neighbor's plants and fish and from doing her home chores every week.

Jamie's expenses were weekly tickets for the Saturday movie matinee, which each [50] cost $4.00. In the middle of the month, Jamie wanted to buy some new computer disks for $6.00, so she studied her budget.

Jamie decided [75] that she could buy the computer disks if she didn't go to one movie matinee. She also remembered that her mother's birthday was the next [100] month. Jamie decided that she would go to only three movie matinees that month. Then, she could buy the computer disks and save the balance of her budget for her mother's birthday gift. [133]

Managing Money

These people are donating some of their surplus
money to a charity that helps animals.

Money Choices

Budgets need to balance. For a budget to balance, expenses need to be equal to or less than income. If expenses are more[25] than income, a person is in debt. If income is more than expenses, a person has a surplus.

A person with a surplus can choose[50] how to use the extra money. Surplus money can be spent, saved, or donated to others. The easiest choice might be to spend extra money[75] immediately. However, if surplus money is saved, a person can buy something of greater value. A person who spends extra money immediately on snacks may[100] never save enough money to buy a skateboard.

Another choice is to donate some money to a worthy cause or charity. There are many charities that help children, animals, and the environment.[132]

Managing Money

This girl is taking out the interest she has earned
by keeping money in her savings account.

Investing Money

A person who leaves $20 in a piggybank for one year will have $20 at the end of the year. Money in a [25] piggybank does not increase in value. To increase in value, money must be invested.

The easiest way to invest money is to deposit it in [50] a savings account at a bank. Banks pay interest on savings accounts. With a 5% interest rate, a $20 deposit will be worth $21 after [75] one year.

Stocks are another kind of investment. A company that needs money can sell shares of its business. These shares are called stocks. Stocks [100] can increase or decrease in value. If a company makes money, a $20 stock might be worth $50 in one year. However, if a company loses money, a $20 stock might be worth $5. [134]

Managing Money

Government revenues help pay for crossing guards,
who help students stay safe as they walk to school.

Government Budgets

Like people, governments have budgets with two parts: income, or revenue, and expenses.

Governments get their revenue from taxes. The U.S. government gets [25] revenue by taxing the income people earn from jobs and from selling goods. Many states get revenue by adding a sales tax when people buy [50] goods. City governments get revenue through property taxes. Property taxes are taxes that are paid every year by people who own houses or stores.

Part [75] of a government's expenses are the services it provides. These services cost money. The U.S. government's expenses include the armed forces. A state government's expenses [100] include roads and schools. A local government's expenses include fire and police services. Like people, governments need to manage their budgets, making sure that their revenues and their expenses balance. [130]

Managing Money

Write words that will help you remember what you learned.

Budgets

_____

_____

_____

_____

Making a Budget

_____

_____

_____

_____

Money Choices

_____

_____

_____

_____

Investing Money

_____

_____

_____

_____

Government Budgets

_____

_____

_____

_____

Budgets

1. A budget is a system for _____

   Ⓐ doing jobs at home or for neighbors.

   Ⓑ saving money.

   Ⓒ earning money in business.

   Ⓓ managing money.

2. Describe the two parts of a budget.

   _____

   _____

   _____

Making a Budget

1. Why does Jamie want to know the difference between her income and her expenses?

   Ⓐ to find out how much money she should spend on fish

   Ⓑ to know how much extra money she has

   Ⓒ to find out how much movie matinees cost

   Ⓓ to make sure she can study her budget

2. How does Jamie plan her budget for the month?

   _____

   _____

   _____

Money Choices

1. Surplus money is money that _____

   Ⓐ is not needed for expenses.

   Ⓑ can be used instead of income and expenses.

   Ⓒ is used for going into debt.

   Ⓓ can be used to make more expenses.

2. Why do budgets need to balance?

   _____

   _____

   _____

Investing Money

1. "Investing Money" is MAINLY about _____

   Ⓐ why you should leave money in a piggybank.

   Ⓑ how to deposit money in a bank.

   Ⓒ why companies sell stocks.

   Ⓓ ways money can increase in value.

2. What are two ways to invest money that you learned about in this passage?

   _____

   _____

   _____

Government Budgets

1. The main idea of "Government Budgets" is that _____

   Ⓐ governments provide services.

   Ⓑ both governments and people have budgets.

   Ⓒ governments invest their money in taxes.

   Ⓓ governments get their revenue from savings.

2. Where do governments get their revenues?

   _____

   _____

   _____

Connect Your Ideas

1. Why do you think it is important to manage money?

   _____

   _____

   _____

2. What are two things you could do if you found that your budget did not balance?

   _____

   _____

   _____

Reading Log • Level E • Book 2

	I Read This	New Words I Learned	New Facts I Learned	What Else I Want to Learn About This Subject
Earth's Moon				
Earth's Satellite				
The Moon and Tides				
A Moon Month				
Humans on the Moon				
The Moons of Other Planets				
Air and the Atmosphere				
Earth's Atmosphere				
Air Pressure				
Sports and Air				
Air and Elevation				
Clean Air				
Minerals				
What Are Minerals?				
Properties of Minerals				
Crystals				
Metals				
Gemstones				

	I Read This	New Words I Learned	New Facts I Learned	What Else I Want to Learn About This Subject
The World's Population				
Why Is Population Important?				
Populations Then and Now				
Where in the World Do People Live?				
Where in the United States Do People Live?				
A Generation of American Children				
Rivers of the United States				
What Is a River?				
Rivers and People				
Rivers and Landscape				
Dams on Rivers				
The Mighty Mississippi				
Managing Money				
Budgets				
Making a Budget				
Money Choices				
Investing Money				
Government Budgets				

Self-Check Graph

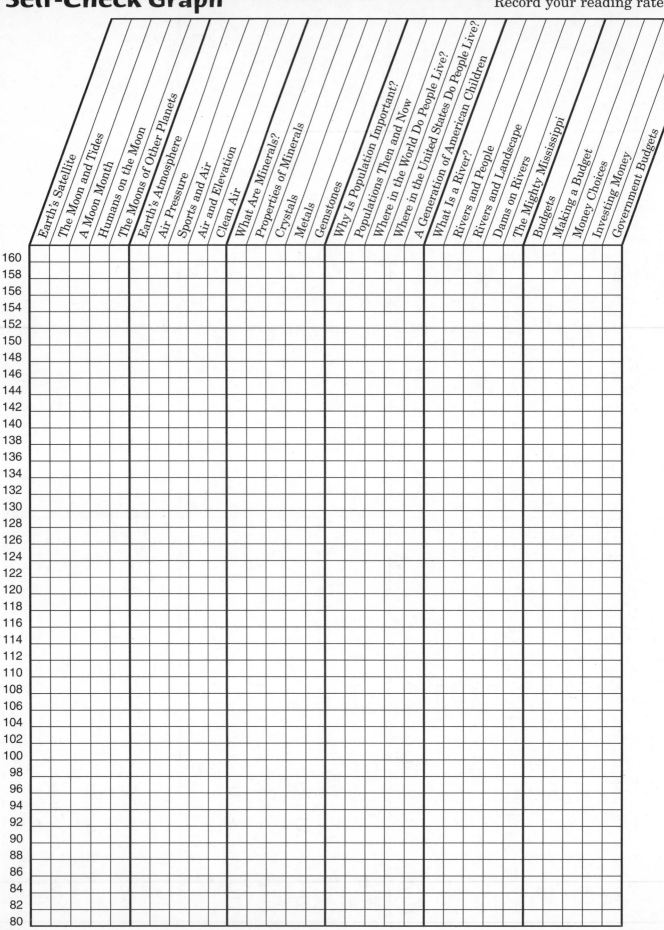

The graph has the following column headers (left to right):

Earth's Satellite · The Moon and Tides · A Moon Month · Humans on the Moon · The Moons of Other Planets · Earth's Atmosphere · Air Pressure · Sports and Air · Air and Elevation · Clean Air · What Are Minerals? · Properties of Minerals · Crystals · Metals · Gemstones · Why Is Population Important? · Populations Then and Now · Where in the World Do People Live? · Where in the United States Do People Live? · A Generation of American Children · What Is a River? · Rivers and People · Rivers and Landscape · Dams on Rivers · The Mighty Mississippi · Budgets · Making a Budget · Money Choices · Investing Money · Government Budgets

The vertical axis values (top to bottom): 160, 158, 156, 154, 152, 150, 148, 146, 144, 142, 140, 138, 136, 134, 132, 130, 128, 126, 124, 122, 120, 118, 116, 114, 112, 110, 108, 106, 104, 102, 100, 98, 96, 94, 92, 90, 88, 86, 84, 82, 80